ASK ORACLE AND LEARN

SARATH KUMAR S

ISBN 979-888591050-7

Contents

Contents

Preface

PL/SQL figures prominently as an enabling technology in almost every new product released by Oracle Corporation. PL/SQL was modeled after Ada,1 a programming language designed for the US Department of Defense. Ada is a high-level language that emphasizes data abstraction, information hiding, and other key elements of modern design strategies. As a result of this very smart design decision by Oracle, PL/SQL is a powerful language that incorporates many of the most advanced elements of procedural languages.

PL/SQL is integrated tightly into Oracle's SQL language: you can execute SQL statements directly from your procedural program without having to rely on any kind of inter- mediate application programming interface (API) such as Java Database Connectivity (JDBC) or Open Database Connectivity (ODBC). Conversely, you can also call your own PL/SQL functions from within a SQL statement.

Oracle developers who want to be successful in the 21st century must learn to use PL/SQL to full advantage. This is a two-step process. First, you must become familiar with and learn how to use the language's ever-expanding set of features; and second, after gaining competence in the individual features, you must learn how to put these constructs together to build complex applications. You don't spend your days and nights writing PL/SQL modules so that you can rise to a higher plane of existence. You use PL/SQL to solve problems for your company or your customers.There is a good deal of code in the book itself, and much more on the accompanying website. In a number of cases, I use the code examples to guide you through the analytical process needed to come up with a solution. In this way you'll see, in the most concrete terms, how to apply PL/ SQL features and undocumented applications of those features to a particular situation.

CHAPTER ONE

Oracle & PL/SQL

Oracle Corporation has a history of leading the software industry in providing declarative, nonprocedural approaches to designing both databases and applications. The Oracle Server technology is among the most advanced, powerful, and stable relational databases in the world. Its application development tools, such as Oracle Forms, Oracle APEX offer high levels of productivity by relying heavily on a "paint your screen" approach in which extensive default capabilities allow developers to avoid heavy customized programming efforts.

If you are completely new to programming or to working with PL/SQL or Oracle Forms/Oracle APEX, learning PL/SQL may seem an intimidating prospect. If this is the case, don't fret! I am confident that you will find it easier than you think. There are mainly two reasons for my optimism:

- Computer languages in general are not that hard to learn, at least compared to a second or third human language. The reason? It's simply that computers are not particularly smart (they "think"—perform operations—rapidly, but not at all creatively). We must rely on a very rigid syntax in order to tell a computer what we want it to do. So the resulting language is also rigid (no exceptions!) and therefore easier for us to pick up.
- PL/SQL truly is an easy language by understanding logic, compared to other programming languages. It relies on a highly structured "block" design with different sections, all identified

with explicit, self-documenting keywords.

CHAPTER TWO

Why PL/SQL?

PL/SQL gives high productivity to programmers as it can query, transform, and update data in a database. PL/SQL allows data manipulation, collection of large volume of data and applying algorithms. Imagine you have to insert 100,000 records every day from a flat file. So are you going to write 100,000 lines of INSERT statements? Or, amongst 100,000 records, you might have some invalid records as per business validation. PL/SQL makes life a lot easier when we are dealing with data, and its one of the easiest languages to learn. PL/SQL is completely portable as code can be executed on any operating system provided Oracle is loaded in it.It offers extensive error checking. Users can write their own customized error handling routines. PL/SQL provides a built-in, integrated programming environment which enhances the performance of transactions with integration to Oracle data dictionary. It also allows free access and sharing of same subprograms by multiple applications.PL/SQL combines the data-manipulating power of SQL with the processing power of procedural languages. You can control program flow with statements like IF and LOOP. As with other procedural programming languages, you can declare variables, define procedures and functions, and trap runtime errors. PL/SQL lets you break complex problems down into easily understandable procedural code, and reuse this code across multiple applications. When a problem can be solved through plain SQL, you can issue SQL commands directly inside your PL/SQL programs, without learning any new APIs. PL/SQL's data types correspond with SQL's column types, making it easy to interchange PL/SQL variables with data inside a table.

Applications written in PL/SQL can run on any operating system and platform where the Oracle database runs. With PL/SQL, you can write portable program libraries and reuse them in different environments.

CHAPTER THREE

Block Structures In PL/SQL

PL/SQL block structure follows divide and conquer approach to solve the problem stepwise.

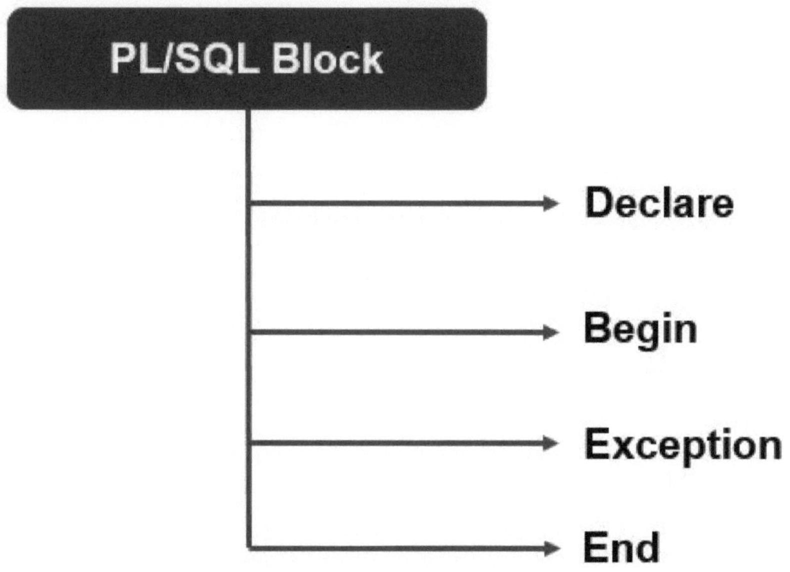

Block Structure

PL/SQL typically organizes the code into blocks. The code block with no name is known as an anonymous block. It is known as the anonymous block because it is not saved in the oracle database. Let us take a look at an anonymous block in PL/SQL.

```
[DECLARE]
declaration statements;
[BEGIN]
execution statements;
[EXCEPTION]
exception statements;
END;
/
```

Looking at the diagram shown above, we can see that the block structure is divided into four parts, i.e declaration, begin, exception and end. Let us try to understand how the block structure works in PL/SQL. Out of all these sections, the execution section is mandatory and rest all are optional.

DECLARE keyword is used to for the declaration section is used to declare data types and structures such as variables, functions, etc.

BEGIN keyword is used for the execution section. It is mandatory and contains all the statements that need to be executed. This block is where the business logic is defined, we can use both procedural or SQL statements in this block.

The **EXCEPTION** keyword is used for the exception section. It contains all the exception statements.

END keyword marks the end of the block and the backward slash '/' tells the tool that you are using(Oracle Database Tool) to execute the PL/SQL block.

Note :

1. BEGIN and END; keyword are compulsory of any PL/SQL program.
2. Whereas DECLARE and EXCEPTION block are optional.

CHAPTER FOUR

Variable Naming & Rules

PL/SQL variable scope is identified the region range which you can reference the variable. The variable in PL/SQL is basically a name that varies or temporary storage location that supports a particular data type. Let us take a look at how we can use the variables in a PL/SQL program.

Variable Naming Rules

PL/SQL follows the following rules for naming variables.

- **The variable cannot be more than 31 characters**
- **The name of the variable should start with an ASCII character. Since PL/SQL is case-sensitive, an uppercase letter and a lowercase letter will be different variables.**
- **After the first character, there has to be a special character($,_) or any number.**

Use the following naming conventions listed below to use the variables.

v_ VARCHAR2

n_ NUMBER

t_ TABLE

r_ ROW

d_ DATE

b_ BOOLEAN

CHAPTER FIVE

Variable Declarations

Let's try to understand how variable declaration is done in PL/SQL

The declaration includes the variable name followed by the data type and separated by a semicolon. Following is an example to show how you can declare a variable in PL/SQL.

```
DECLARE
v_name VARCHAR(25);
n_age NUMBER(3);
BEGIN
NULL;
END;
```

You can also add the length of the data type as we have done in the example above.

CHAPTER SIX

Variable Anchors

The anchor basically refers to the use of the %TYPE keyword that to declare a variable with the data type associated with a column's data type of a particular column in a table.

Take a look at an example to understand this. Suppose we have a table EMPLOYEES, we can use the anchors in the following way.

```
DECLARE
v_name EMPLOYEE.NAME%TYPE;
n_age EMPLOYEE.AGE%TYPE;
BEGIN
NULL;
END;
/
```

CHAPTER SEVEN

Variable Assignments

Variable assignment is quite easy, we can use the assignment operator to assign values to a variable. The following example shows how we can assign values to a variable.

```
DECLARE
v_name VARCHAR(20);
n_course VARCHAR(10);
BEGIN
v_name = "Sarath Kumar S";
v_course = "M.TECH";
END;
/
```

CHAPTER EIGHT

Variable Initializations

We can initialize a value for the variable in the declaration section too. The following example shows how we can initialize values to a variable.

```
DECLARE
v_name VARCHAR(20) = "Sarath Kumar S";
n_course VARCHAR(10) = "M.TECH";
BEGIN
NULL;
END;
/
```

Now that we know how we can work with the variables, let us try to understand how we will use functions in PL/SQL.

CHAPTER NINE

Function In PL/SQL

A function in PL/SQL is basically a named block that returns a value. You can store the function as database object and we can reuse that object in multiple PL SQL blocks. The function always called as a part of expression or it is used to provide the parameter value, the following syntax shows how we can use functions in PL/SQL.

```
CREATE [OR REPLACE] FUNCTION function_name [(
parameter_1 [IN] [OUT] data_type,
parameter_2 [IN] [OUT] data_type,
parameter_N [IN] [OUT] data_type]
RETURN return_data_type IS
BEGIN
statements
return return_data_type;
EXCEPTION
END;
/
```

First of all, you must specify a function name after the keyword. The function name has to start with a verb. A function may have none, one or more parameters that we specify in parameters. We have to specify the data type of each parameter explicitly, and then comes the mode which can either of the following.

IN – The IN parameter is a read-only parameter.

OUT – It is a write-only parameter

IN OUT – The IN OUT parameter is both read-write parameter.

Here is a simple example to show how we use functions in PL/SQL.

```
CREATE OR REPLACE FUNCTION try_parse(
iv_number IN VARCHAR2)
RETURN NUMBER IS
BEGIN
RETURN to_number(iv_number);
EXCEPTION
WHEN others THEN
RETURN NULL;
END;
```

Calling A Function

Let us try to call the function that we have made in an anonymous block in the following example.

```
SET SERVEROUTPUT ON SIZE 1000000;
DECLARE
n_x number;
n_y number;
n_z number;
BEGIN
n_x := try_parse('256');
n_y := try_parse('29.72');
n_z := try_parse('pqrs');
DBMS_OUTPUT.PUT_LINE(n_x);
DBMS_OUTPUT.PUT_LINE(n_y);
DBMS_OUTPUT.PUT_LINE(n_z);
END;
/
```

We can call the function in a SELECT statement too.

CHAPTER TEN

Advantages of Functions

In this section we can see multiple advantages of functions in PL/SQL :

Reduce Complexity : When there are complex or awkward activities we can write a function and easily can capture those activities.

Increase Efficiency : The second advantage of using function is to increase efficiency.

Reusability : We can easily reuse the functions in PL/SQL so reusability is another advantage of using function.

Data Manipulation : We can use functions to easily manipulate the data.

Now that we know how we can use functions in PL/SQL and multiple advantages of using it , let us try to understand how we work with procedures in PL/SQL.

CHAPTER ELEVEN

PL/SQL Procedure

A procedure is basically a block that does a specific task. Using a procedure we can wrap or encapsulate complex business logic and reuse them in both application and database layer.

Let us take a look at a simple example to understand how the procedure works in PL/SQL.

```
CREATE OR REPLACE PROCEDURE adjust_salary(
in_employee_id IN EMPLOYEES.EMPLOYEE_ID%TYPE,
in_percent IN NUMBER
) IS
BEGIN
-- update employee's salary
UPDATE employees
SET salary = salary + salary * in_percent / 100
WHERE employee_id = in_employee_id;
END;
```

In the above example, we have two parameters, the procedure adjusts the salary by a given percentage and the UPDATE keyword updates the value in the salary information.

Procedure Header

The section before the keyword IS is called the procedure header. The following are a few pointers one must be familiar with while working with procedures.

schema – It is the optional name of the schema that the procedure belongs to.

name – The name of the procedure which should start with a verb.

parameters – It is the optional list of parameters.

AUTHID – It determines whether the procedure will execute with the privilege of the current user or the original owner of the procedure.

Procedure Body

Everything that comes after the IS keyword is called the procedure body. We have the declaration, exception and execution statements in the procedure body. Unlike the function, the RETURN keyword in a procedure is used to halt the execution and return the control to the caller.

Calling A Procedure

Let us see how we can call a procedure in PL/SQL.

EXEC procedure_name(param1,param2...paramN);

We can call the procedures with no parameters with just using the EXEC keyword and procedure name. Now that we know how we can work with procedures, let us try to understand how nested blocks are used in PL/SQL.

CHAPTER TWELVE

Advantages of Procedures

Stored procedures provide some crucial benefits, which are:

- **Reusable**: Talking about saving time, developers do not have worry about writing queries multiple times in applications. Store Procedures allow developers to write SQL statements once and use them repeatedly and share the data multiple times on a distributed environment.

- **Easy to modify**: You can quickly change the statements in a stored procedure as and when you want to, with the help of the ALTER TABLE command.

- **Security**: One very useful accepts of using a stored procedures is the security cover it provides to its data source. Since there are no direct accesses to the tables, it prevents unauthorized manipulation of records inside the tables. A properly written procedure acts as a solid deterrence to SQL injections. SQL injections are a combination of SQL statements and techniques that can break into databases and do unauthorized manipulation to the data.
- **Low network traffic**: The server only passes the procedure name instead of the whole query, reducing network traffic.
- **Increases performance**: Upon the first use, a plan for the stored procedure is created and stored in the buffer pool for quick execution for the next time.

CHAPTER THIRTEEN

Nested Block

A nested block is nothing but a combination of one or more PL/SQL blocks to get better control over the execution and exceptional handling for the program.

Here is a simple example of a nested block.

```
SET SERVEROUTPUT ON SIZE 1000000;
DECLARE
n_emp_id EMPLOYEES.EMPLOYEE_ID%TYPE := &emp_id1;
BEGIN
DECLARE
n_emp_id employees.employee_id%TYPE := &emp_id2;
v_name employees.first_name%TYPE;
BEGIN
SELECT first_name
INTO v_name
FROM employees
WHERE employee_id = n_emp_id;
DBMS_OUTPUT.PUT_LINE('First name of employee ' ||
n_emp_id ||
' is ' || v_name);
EXCEPTION
WHEN no_data_found THEN
DBMS_OUTPUT.PUT_LINE('Employee ' || n_emp_id || ' not
found');
END;
END;
```

```
/
```

The outer PL/SQL block in the above example is known as the parent block or enclosing block, the inner block, on the other hand, is known as the child block or the enclosed block.

It is not a great idea to use the variables with the same names in both the blocks because during the execution the child block variable will override the parent block variable. It happens because PL/SQL gives first priority to the variable inside its own block.

CHAPTER FOURTEEN

Block Label

We can overcome this issue with the block label that helps us make references to variables inside blocks using a label.

Here is a simple example to show how we can use a block label.

```
<<block_label>>
DECLARE
...
BEGIN
...
END;
```

Using a block label helps to improve the readability of the code, gain better control and make references to the blocks. Now that we know how we can work with nested blocks, let us try to understand how the IF STATEMENT works in PL/SQL.

CHAPTER FIFTEEN

IF Statement

PL/SQL has three IF STATEMENTS

IF-THEN – It is the simplest IF STATEMENT if the condition is true the statements will execute, if the condition is false, it does nothing.

IF-THEN-ELSE – In this, the ELSE clause is added for an alternative sequence of statements.

IF-THEN-ELSEIF – It allows us to execute multiple test conditions in a sequence

IF-THEN Syntax

IF condition THEN

sequence_of_statements;

END IF;

IF-THEN-ELSE Syntax

IF condition THEN

sequence_of_if_statements;

ELSE

sequence_of_else_statements;

END IF;

IF-THEN-ELSEIF Syntax

IF condition1 THEN

sequence_of_statements1

ELSIF condition2 THEN

sequence_of_statements2

ELSE

sequence_of_statements3

END IF;

Now that we are done with the IF STATEMENT let us look at the CASE statement in PL/SQL.

CHAPTER SIXTEEN

CASE Statement

The CASE statement basically helps in executing a sequence of statements based on a selector. A selector, in this case, can be anything, it can be a variable, function or a simple expression. Here is a simple example to show the syntax of the CASE statement in PL/SQL.

```
[<<label_name>>]
CASE [TRUE | selector]
WHEN expression1 THEN
sequence_of_statements1;
WHEN expression2 THEN
sequence_of_statements2;
...
WHEN expressionN THEN
sequence_of_statementsN;
[ELSE sequence_of_statementsN+1;]
END CASE [label_name];
```

In the above syntax, after the CASE keyword comes the selector. PL/SQL will evaluate the selector only once to determine which statement needs to be executed.

Followed by the selector is the WHEN keyword. If the expression satisfies the selector then the corresponding statement after THEN keyword gets executed.

Now that we know how we can use a CASE statement, let us try to understand how we will use the loop statements in the PL/SQL.

CHAPTER SEVENTEEN

Loop Statement

A loop statement in PL/SQL is an iterative statement that allows you to execute a sequence of statements multiple times. Here is a simple example to show the syntax of a loop statement in PL/SQL.

```
LOOP
sequence_of_statements;
END LOOP;
```

There has to be at least one executable statement in between the LOOP and END LOOP keyword.

Loop with EXIT Statement

The EXIT and EXIT when statements allow you exit the loop. EXIT WHEN statement terminates the loop conditionally while EXIT terminates the execution unconditionally.

```
LOOP
...
EXIT WHEN condition;
END LOOP;
```

Loop Label

A loop label is used to qualify the name of the loop counter variable when used in a nested loop. Following is the syntax of a loop label.

```
<<label>>
LOOP
sequence_of_statements;
END LOOP label;
```

Now that we know how we can use the loop statements let us take a look at while loop statements for better understanding.

While Loop Statement

We can use the WHILE loop statement when the number of executions are not defined until the execution starts. The following syntax is used for a WHILE loop statement in PL/SQL.

```
WHILE condition
LOOP
sequence_of_statements;
END LOOP;
```

The condition in the syntax is a boolean value or expression that evaluates to be either TRUE, FALSE or NULL. If the condition is TRUE, the statements will be executed, if it is FALSE, the execution stops and the control goes to the next executable statement.

Now that we know how we can use a WHILE loop statement, let us take a look at the FOR loop statement.

For Loop Statement

A FOR loop statement in PL/SQL allows us to execute a sequence of statements for a definite number of times. Following is the syntax to use FOR loop statement in PL/SQL.

```
FOR loop_counter IN [REVERSE] lower_bound .. higher_bound
LOOP
sequence_of_statements;
END LOOP;
```

PL/SQL creates a local variable loop_counter automatically with an INTEGER data type for the loop so that you don't have to declare it explicitly. The lowerbound..higherbound is the range over which the loop iterates. Also, you must have at least one executable statement between LOOP and END LOOP keywords.

Now that we know how we can use the loop statements in PL/SQL, let us take a look at exceptional handling in PL/SQL.

CHAPTER EIGHTEEN

PL/SQL Collections

A collection is a group of elements of homogenous data types. It generally comprises arrays, lists, sets, and so on. Each of the elements has a particular subscript which reflects its position.

PL/SQL collections are generally used for storage and manipulation of big chunks of data, using the keyword **BULK COLLECT** in Oracle. A bulk collection is a method of getting data when the PL/SQL engine informs the SQL engine to accumulate multiple rows at once and store them in a collection. The bulk collect enhances the performance by cutting down the interaction between the PL/SQL engine and database.

The following collection types are available in PL/SQL:

Index-by-tables: Associative arrays, often known as index-by tables, allow you to look up elements by subscribing them with arbitrary numbers and strings. In other programming languages, hash tables are comparable to this.

Nested tables: An arbitrary amount of elements can be stored in nested tables. As subscripts, they use consecutive numerals. Equivalent SQL types can be defined, allowing nested tables to be stored in database tables and manipulated via SQL.

Varray: Variable-size arrays are also called as varrays, have a set number of elements that they can carry. As subscripts, they use consecutive numerals. Equivalent SQL types can be defined, allowing varrays to be stored in database tables. They can be saved and retrieved using SQL, but their versatility is limited compared to stacked tables.

In short we can summarize that the **nested tables can store a random number of elements. Varrays can store a fixed number of elements** and the **associative arrays allow us to search elements with random numbers and strings.**

CHAPTER NINETEEN

Index-By-Tables

The index-by table is commonly called the associative array. In terms of structure, both the index-by table and nested tables are similar and have subscript to access the elements.

An associative array is represented by a key-value pair. Each of the unique keys is used to identify the value in the array. The data type of the key can be a string or an integer defined while creating it. A key is added to the index-by table by simply assigning a value for the first time. To modify the same entry, we have to use the same key.

The key should be a unique one either as a primary key in a table or by combining strings together to develop unique value. This type of collection has an array size that is dynamic and has either sparse or dense characteristics. One difference between the index-by table and the nested table is that the former cannot be stored in the column of the database but the nested table can be stored.

The associative arrays provide easy maintenance of subscript and are created within a PL/SQL block. It is like a SQL table where values are obtained with the help of the primary key. This is generally used for temporary data storage and can be used instead of SQL tables for avoiding network traffic and disk storage required by SQL tables.

As the associative arrays do not store persistent data, they cannot be used with SQL statements like SELECT and INSERT. However, they can be made unending for a session of the database by declaring their data type as a package and defining them inside the body of the package.

Syntax of the index-by table:

```
TYPE type IS TABLE OF element [NOT NULL]
INDEX BY [BINARY_INTEGER | PLS_INTEGER | VARCHAR2(size)];
INDEX BY key;
```

Here, the 'key' is numeric. It can be either BINARY_INTEGER or PLS_INTEGER. Its datatype can be varchar, varchar2, long, or string. The varchar based key should be mentioned with length.

'element' is the data type.

'size' is the maximum number of elements. It is a positive integer.

'type' is the type specifier.

Code implementation with the index-by table:

```
DECLARE
TYPE age IS TABLE OF NUMBER INDEX BY VARCHAR(25);
age_empl age;
employee VARCHAR(25);
BEGIN
-- adding employee details to the table
age_empl('Sam') := 30;
age_empl('Venu') := 35;
-- printing the table contents in the console
employee := age_empl.FIRST;
WHILE employee IS NOT null LOOP
dbms_output.put_line
('Employee name is ' || employee || ' and age is ' || TO_CHAR(age_empl(employee)));
employee := age_empl.NEXT(employee);
END LOOP;
END;
/
```

CHAPTER TWENTY

Nested Tables

The nested tables are like a single column database table or a 1-dimensional array where the array size is dynamic. Its subscript is of numeric type. We can get the nested table into a variable by giving the rows a subscript that begins with 1. This feature makes it similar in nature like an array.

A nested table can be held in a column of a database. It can also be used for manipulating SQL operations by joining tables. Since it is like a dynamic array so the upper limit can be of any size.

A nested table can have both dense and sparse collection characteristics which means any element can be deleted randomly (making it sparse) with the help of the DELETE procedure. The deletion of data causes a discontinuity in the index but the NEXT function helps to iterate to the next subscripts. Since the data is stored in the form of a table, it can be retrieved with the help of SELECT statements.

A nested table can be built at the schema level or in PL/SQL block. It is like a database object which is accessible within the database or subprogram.

Syntax of the nested table:

TYPE <<type>> IS TABLE OF <<element>> [NOT NULL];

Here, 'type' is the type specifier. 'element' is the data type.

Code implementation with the nested table:

```
DECLARE
TYPE subject IS TABLE OF VARCHAR(15);
TYPE teacher IS TABLE OF VARCHAR2(20);
```

```
subjectnames subject;
subjectteacher teacher;
summ integer;
BEGIN
-- adding subject and its teachers to the table
subjectnames := subject('PLSQL', 'SELENIUM', 'JMETER');
subjectteacher:= teacher('Sashi', 'Mala', 'Mukund');
-- returns count of number of elements in nested table
summ:= subjectteacher.count;
-- printing the content to the console
dbms_output.put_line('Total Number of Teachers: '|| summ);
FOR i IN 1 .. summ LOOP
dbms_output.put_line('Subject:'||subjectnames(i)||', Teacher:' ||
subjectteacher(i));
end loop;
END
```

CHAPTER TWENTY-ONE

Varray

The Varrays store a fixed number of elements and are like a one-dimensional array. However, the number of elements can be modified at runtime. It is a consecutive set of elements of similar data types. It can be stored in a database table that can be handled with the help of SQL statements. But the process is not as easy and flexible as in a nested table.

The maximum size of Varray is defined in its type definition. It has a one after another memory arrangement beginning with 1 subscript and the lowest location address points to the starting element and the highest location address points to the end element. All the elements of a Varray are identified with an index.

This type of collection has numeric subscript and has dense characteristics. Thus the array elements cannot be deleted in between. Either the entire Varray should be deleted or its end can be trimmed. Due to its dense characteristics, it has less flexibility of use.

The Varray can be created either within a PL/SQL block or at the level of schema. It is treated as a database object which can be accessed within the database or within a subprogram. Varray is used more frequently when the size of the array is known to us. It should be initialized prior to using them and it can be initialized with the help of a constructor. Its value is NULL when declared and should be initialized before referencing its elements.

Syntax of Varray:

TYPE <<type>> IS {VARRAY | VARYING ARRAY} (<<size>>) OF <<element>> [NOT NULL];

Here,

'type' is the type specifier.

'element' is the data type.

'size' is the maximum number of elements in an array. It is a positive integer.

Varray Variables Declaration And Initialization

After creating a Varray, we can declare it in the way described below:

Syntax:

name type_n [:= type_n(...)];

Here,

'name' is the Varray name.

'type_n' is the type of Varray.

'type_n(...)' is the constructor of type Varray. The argument lists are mentioned by a comma separator and of type Varray.

We have to initialize a Varray variable before using it else it gives uninitialized collection error. The initialization is done in the way described below.

Syntax:

name type_n := type_n();

This will initialize the variable with zero elements. In order to populate elements in the varray variables, the syntax is:

name type_n := type_n(e1, e2, ...);

Code implementation with Varray:

```
DECLARE
type countrynames IS VARRAY(3) OF VARCHAR2(50);
type currency IS VARRAY(3) OF VARCHAR2(15);
country countrynames;
cur currency;
addition integer;
BEGIN
-- adding country and its currency to the table
country := countrynames('INDIA', 'USA', 'UK');
```

```
cur:= currency('INR', 'DOLLAR', 'POUND');
-- returns count of number of countries in varray
addition := country.count;
-- printing the content to the console
dbms_output.put_line('Total Number of countries : '||
addition);
FOR i in 1 .. addition LOOP
dbms_output.put_line('Country: ' || country(i) ||
' ,Currency : ' || cur(i));
END LOOP;
END;
/
```

CHAPTER TWENTY-TWO

PL/SQL Records

A record is a collection of data objects that are kept in fields, each having its own name and datatype. Records are made up of a collection of fields that are similar to the columns in a row. You can declare a PL/SQL record that resembles a row in a database table without listing all the columns using the % ROWTYPE attribute. Even when columns are added to the table, your code continues to work. You can build a view or declare a cursor to choose the right columns and perform any necessary joins, then apply percent ROWTYPE to the view or cursor to represent a subset of columns in a table or columns from separate tables.

You need to define a RECORD type and then declare records of the same type to generate records. You may also utilize the percent ROWTYPE property to construct a matching record by creating or finding a table, view, or PL/SQL cursor with the data you desire.

RECORD types can be defined in the declarative section of any PL/SQL block, subprogram, or package. You can put a NOT NULL constraint on fields or give them default values when creating your own RECORD type.

Here is an example for declaring and Initializing a Simple Record Type

```
DECLARE
TYPE DeptRecTyp IS RECORD (
deptid NUMBER(4) NOT NULL := 99,
dname departments.department_name%TYPE,
loc departments.location_id%TYPE,
```

```
region regions%ROWTYPE );
dept_rec DeptRecTyp;
BEGIN
dept_rec.dname := 'buying';
END;
/
```

CHAPTER TWENTY-THREE

Cursors

Cursor is an database object and retrieve the rows from database row by row,it is mainly use for ot reduce the network traffic.In addition to traversing records in a database, cursors also facilitate data retrieval, adding and deleting records.

A cursor needs to be declared and assigned a name, before it could be used.

There are 5 features

(i)DECLARE the cursor

(ii)OPEN the cursor

(iii)FETCH the cursor

(iv)CLOSE the cursor

(v)DEALLOCATE the cursor

Cursor needs to be opened using the OPEN command.This operation would place the cursor just before the first row of the result set of records. Then the cursor has to perform the FETCH operation to actually get a row of data in to the application. Finally, the cursor has to be closed using the CLOSE operation. Closed cursors can be opened again.

Ex : DECLARE employee_cursor CURSOR FOR SELECT * FROM employee OPEN employee_cursor FETCH NEXT FROM employee_cursor

Here We declaring the cursor named “employee_cursor”, which has the values of “SELECT * FROM employee”.

CHAPTER TWENTY-FOUR

Triggers

Triggers in oracle are blocks of PL/SQL code which oracle engine can execute automatically based on some action or event.

These events can be:

DDL statements (CREATE, ALTER, DROP, TRUNCATE)

DML statements (INSERT, SELECT, UPDATE, DELETE)

Database operation like connecting or disconnecting to oracle (LOGON, LOGOFF, SHUTDOWN)

Triggers are automatically and repeatedly called upon by oracle engine on satisfying certain condition.

Triggers can be activated or deactivated depending on the requirements.

If triggers are activated then they are executed implicitly by oracle engine and if triggers are deactivated then they are executed explicitly by oracle engine.

Here we have mentioned a few use cases where using triggers proves very helpful:

- Maintaining complex constraints which is either impossible or very difficult via normal constraint(like primary, foreign, unique etc) applying technique.
- Recording the changes made on the table.
- Automatically generating primary key values.
- Prevent invalid transactions to occur.
- Granting authorization and providing security to database.
- Enforcing referential integrity.

Triggers can be classified into three categories:

1. Level Triggers
2. Event Triggers
3. Timing Triggers

which are further divided into different parts.

Level Triggers

There are 2 different types of level triggers, they are:

ROW LEVEL TRIGGERS

It fires for every record that got affected with the execution of DML statements like INSERT, UPDATE, DELETE etc.

It always use a FOR EACH ROW clause in a triggering statement.

STATEMENT LEVEL TRIGGERS

It fires once for each statement that is executed.

Event Triggers

There are 3 different types of event triggers, they are:

DDL EVENT TRIGGER

It fires with the execution of every DDL statement(CREATE, ALTER, DROP, TRUNCATE).

DML EVENT TRIGGER

It fires with the execution of every DML statement(INSERT, UPDATE, DELETE).

DATABASE EVENT TRIGGER

It fires with the execution of every database operation which can be LOGON, LOGOFF, SHUTDOWN, SERVERERROR etc.

Timing Triggers

There are 2 different types of timing triggers, they are:

BEFORE TRIGGER

- It fires before executing DML statement.
- Triggering statement may or may not executed depending upon the before condition block.

AFTER TRIGGER

- It fires after executing DML statement

Following is the syntax for creating a trigger:

```
CREATE OR REPLACE TRIGGER <trigger_name>
BEFORE/AFTER/INSTEAD OF
INSERT/DELETE/UPDATE ON <table_name>
REFERENCING (OLD AS O, NEW AS N)
FOR EACH ROW WHEN (test_condition)
DECLARE
-- Variable declaration;
BEGIN
-- Executable statements;
EXCEPTION
-- Error handling statements;
END <trigger_name>;
END;
```

Below we have a simple program to demonstrate the use of Triggers in PL/SQL code block.

```
CREATE OR REPLACE TRIGGER CheckAge
BEFORE
INSERT OR UPDATE ON student
FOR EACH ROW
BEGIN
IF :new.Age>30 THEN
raise_application_error(-20001, 'Age should not be greater than
30');
END IF;
END;
```

CHAPTER TWENTY-FIVE

Materialized Views

In general, a view represents a queries result set. When this query result is cached and updated from the base table's periodically, it is called as a materialized view. It is most commonly used in scenarios where frequent query data needs to be accessed. Unlike a view, materialized view is not virtual. It is typically used in data warehousing. Using materialized view network load is reduced.

Materialized Views are automatically updated as their base tables are updated. Security can be better controlled in a materialized view rather than a table.

Why use materialized view instead of a table?

Materialized views are basically used to increase query performance since it contains results of a query. They should be used for reporting instead of a table for a faster execution.

One of the biggest benefit of using a materialized view is that Oracle takes care of keeping the data in sync. If you have a separate aggregate table, you are responsible for keeping the data synchronized. That generally requires a reasonable amount of code and a decent amount of testing and most organizations manage to make mistakes that leave holes that cause the aggregate table to get out of sync. This is particularly true when you try to implement incremental refreshes of the aggregate table.

Another major benefit is that, depending on the settings, Oracle can use query rewrite to use materialized views when users issue queries against base tables. So, for example, if you have a bunch of existing reports against a detail table that produce daily, monthly, and yearly aggregate results, you can create a materialized view on the base table that aggregates the data at a daily level and the optimizer can utilize that materialized view for all your existing queries. This makes it much easier to optimize reporting workloads in a data warehouse without trying to go and rewrite dozens of reports to use your new aggregate table or to mess with DBMS_ADVANCED_REWRITE to force your own rewrites of the queries.

CHAPTER TWENTY-SIX

Exceptional Handling

In PL/SQL any kind of error is treated as an exception. An exception can be treated as a special condition that can change or alter the execution flow. In PL/SQL, there are two types of exceptions.

- System Exception – It is raised by the PL/SQL run-time when it detects an error.
- Programmer-Defined Exception – These exceptions are defined by the programmer in a specific application.

Defining An Exception

Any abnormal condition or event that interrupts the normal flow of our program instructions at run time or in simple words an exception is an error. An exception in PL/SQL has to be declared before it can be raised. We can define the exception using the EXCEPTION keyword like we have done in the example below.

Syntax of Exception Handling in PL/SQL

```
DECLARE
<declarations section>
BEGIN
<executable command(s)>
EXCEPTION
<exception handling goes here >
WHEN exception1 THEN
exception1-handling-statements
```

```
WHEN exception2 THEN
exception2-handling-statements
WHEN exception3 THEN
exception3-handling-statements
........
WHEN others THEN
exception3-handling-statements
END;
```

Guidelines for Avoiding and Handling PL/SQL Errors and Exceptions

- Add exception handlers whenever there is any possibility of an error occurring.
- Add error-checking code whenever you can predict that an error might occur if your code gets bad input data.
- Make your programs robust enough to work even if the database is not in the state you expect.
- Handle named exceptions whenever possible, instead of using WHEN OTHERS in exception handlers.
- Test your code with different combinations of bad data to see what potential errors arise.
- Write out debugging information in your exception handlers.

Using PRAGMA EXCEPTION_INIT function

In the PRAGMA EXCEPTION_INIT function, an exception name is associated with an Oracle error number. This name can be used in designing the exception handler for the error. For huge projects with many user defined errors, PRAGMA EXCEPTION_INIT is the most useful and suitable method.

Syntax

```
DECLARE
deadlock_detected EXCEPTION;
PRAGMA EXCEPTION_INIT(deadlock_detected, -60);
BEGIN
NULL; -- Some operation that causes an ORA-00060 error
```

```
EXCEPTION
WHEN deadlock_detected THEN
NULL; -- handle the error
END;
```

The PRAGMA EXCEPTION_INIT tells the compiler to associate an exception name with an Oracle error number as mentioned earlier. It lets you refer to any internal exception by name and write a specific handler for it. When you see an error stack, or sequence of error messages, the one on top is the one that can be trapped and handled.

CHAPTER TWENTY-SEVEN

PL/SQL Packages

A package is an encapsulated collection of related program objects (for example, procedures, functions, variables, constants, cursors, and exceptions) stored together in the database.

Using packages is an alternative to creating procedures and functions as standalone schema objects. Packages have many advantages over standalone procedures and functions. For example, they:

- Let you organize your application development more efficiently.
- Let you grant privileges more efficiently.
- Let you modify package objects without recompiling dependent schema objects.
- Enable Oracle Database to read multiple package objects into memory at once.
- Can contain global variables and cursors that are available to all procedures and functions in the package.
- Let you overload procedures or functions. Overloading a procedure means creating multiple procedures with the same name in the same package, each taking arguments of different number or datatype.

The PL SQL packages always have two parts :

- Package Specification
- Package body

The specification part of a package declares the public types, variables, constants, and subprograms that are visible outside the immediate scope of the package. The body of a package defines the objects declared in the specification, as well as private objects that are not visible to applications outside the package.

Syntax for package specification :

Create or Replace Package package_name is/as

Public type and variable declaration;

subprogram specification;

End package_name;

Syntax for package body:

Create or Replace package body package_name is/as

All business code for variable declaration and subprograms exact code;

Begin

Business Logic;

End;

CHAPTER TWENTY-EIGHT

Effective Coding Strategies

1. Use UPPER-lower case method to make code more readable.
2. Use consistent indentation.
3. Avoid hard-coded literals of any kind in your programs.
4. Make sure your name describes the module accurately.
5. Test all of your assumptions as you debug your code.
6. Use anchored declarations whenever possible.
7. Streamline your code with records.
8. Take advantage of the cursor FOR loop.
9. Enhance scope control with nested blocks.
10. Use Self-identifying Parameters
11. Avoid unstructured exits from loops.
12. Optimize foreign key lookups with PL/SQL tables.
13. Construct abstract data types with PL/SQL packages.
14. Code a single RETURN for successful function execution.
15. Handle exceptions clearly throughout the code (Exception Handling) with proper comments.

CHAPTER TWENTY-NINE

Query Optimization Techniques

Here are the query optimization techniques in oracle which you could use to performance tune your Oracle database:

1. Start with the System Level SQL tuning

To get started with the SQL query optimization it is important that you perform SQL tuning at the System level first else other changes might get undo automatically leading to rework in performance tuning.

2. Rewrite complex subqueries with temporary tables

You can easily rewrite complex subqueries in Oracle SQL with Global Temporary Table (GTT) and SQL WITH operator. This is helpful in complex subqueries such as WHERE clause subqueries, SELECT clause scalar subqueries and FROM clause in-line views.

Upon tuning with the queries with temporary tables and WITH clause,the performance of the SQL query in Oracle increases by many folds.

3. Index all predicates

For a high performance and scalability, Index all predicates of JOIN, WHERE, ORDER BY and GROUP BY clauses in SQL queries. In absence of the proper indexing, it causes table scanning of SQL queries which consequently results in performance or locking issues.

Thus, it is good to have all predicates indexed except where the column data has low cardinality.

4. Use Inner Joins instead of Outer Joins

Use outer join only if it is very necessary, otherwise, try replacing it with inner joins for a better SQL query performance. As outer joins slower the SQL execution, thereby affecting optimization, thus using inner joins is highly advisable for better performance.

5. Use CLOB/BLOB columns at end statements

Oracle 10g and Oracle 11g require CLOB/BLOB columns at the end statements, else it might result in an execution failure when the input value size is more than 1000 characters.

Oracle Query Optimization Tool

Oracle Query Optimization Tool (The Query Optimizer), is a built-in database software which helps in the optimization of SQL queries in Oracle, by finding out the most efficient method in which a SQL query can access data from an Oracle database.

It generates multiple possible Execution plans along with costs involve for a query and compares them to find out the most feasible plan to boost up overall database performance. It takes Query blocks, which is a parsed representation of the SQL statement as the input and based on the statistics tell the most feasible execution plan as a result.

This way Oracle Query Optimization Tool helps in getting the most feasible and cost-effective execution plan for the SQL queries in your Oracle database.

In a nutshell

Query Optimization is very important for a healthy and high performing Oracle database. Using the above techniques could be very useful in Optimizing SQL queries Oracle by fastening the execution. At the same, Oracle Query Optimization Tool could largely help to figure out the most feasible execution plan for the queries boosting up the performance and making it more cost effective.

A diligent database administrator could very well use the above techniques the Query Optimizer to enable a high functioning database. At OptimizDBA, we are dedicated to making your database highly optimized by using the advanced techniques and due diligence with our expert and experienced team of Database Administrators. Feel free to contact us and we will be obliged to assist you in optimizing your database.

CHAPTER THIRTY

Oracle Tools

A few of the most used tools developed by Oracle Corporation are mentioned below.

1) **Oracle APEX**

Oracle APEX is an enterprise low-code development platform from Oracle Corporation that is used to develop and deploy web applications on Oracle databases. Using APEX, developers can quickly develop and deploy compelling apps that solve real problems and provide immediate value. You won't need to be an expert in a vast array of technologies to deliver sophisticated solutions. Focus on solving the problem with PL/SQL and let APEX take care of the rest.

2) **OracleSQL Developer**

This is another free of cost tool that allows developers to leverage their SQL & PL/SQL skills by developing software applications. It allows programmers to browse through database objects within a tree-like structure, execute SQL commands and scripts, debug the code, and other administrative tasks.

3) **Java Based Tools**

Oracle gives users an option, to develop applications that could be based out of Java and PL/SQL, using the below tools.

- **Oracle JDeveloper**
- **Oracle Forms**
- **Oracle Reports**

4) **Oracle Rest Data Services (ORDS)**

ORDS is a Java-based, a middle-tier application that helps programmers develop REST interfaces for data available in Oracle Database. It allows mapping of DB transactions with HTTP(s) methods like POST, GET, PUT, etc. and results would be returned in JSON format.

5) **Oracle Database Upgrade Assistant (DBUA)**

This tool provides an interface which supports database upgrade.

6) **Oracle OPatch**

Using Oracle OPatch, interim patches can be applied to Oracle software. If required, the applied patch can be rolled back too, using the Opatch tool.

7) **Oracle SQLTXPLAIN**

It is again free of cost tool, developed by Oracle that facilitates tuning of Oracle SQL code.

Printed by Libri Plureos GmbH in Hamburg,
Germany